delicate machinery suspended

poems

a n n e   m .   d o e   o v e r s t r e e t

ts T. S. Poetry Press • New York

T. S. Poetry Press
Ossining, New York
Tspoetry.com

Throughout this collection, various pieces contain references to the following
brands and sources: Tide detergent is a product of Proctor and Gamble;
Bazooka gum is a registered trademark of The Topps Company, Inc.; Ryvita
crackers/crispbread are a product of The Jordans and Ryvita Company
Limited; *Planet Earth* is a Discovery Channel series.

Cover image by Claire M. Burge claireburge.com

ISBN 978-0-9845531-5-0

Library of Congress Cataloging-in-Publication Data:
Overstreet, Anne M. Doe
    [Poems.]
    Delicate Machinery Suspended: Poems/Anne M. Doe Overstreet
    ISBN 978-0-9845531-5-0
    Library of Congress Control Number: 2011929965

The author and publisher wish to express their grateful acknowledgment to
the following publications and venues in which versions of these poems first
appeared or are forthcoming:

Asheville Poetry Review: Preparing For Market. *Nimrod International Prose and Poetry
Journal:* A Case for Insomnia. *DMQ Review:* Dog Night, The Bearded Lady
Asleep, Surviving the Open Heart. *Radix:* Rental, Sour Plums. *Relief:* Annuncia-
tion Triptych, In This Place of Grass. *Cranky:* Red # 9. *Talking River Review:* Men
Who Love the Domed Heads of Old Dogs. *TheMatthewsHouseProject.com:* This
Has Been a Summer of Moths. *Soul Food Reading Series:* Soufflé. Seattle City
Council's *Word's Worth Series:* Shade Half Drawn.

To, as always, my beloved Jeffrey,
with whom much is possible

Contents

I. Compass

II. Delicate Work

III. How to Fall

IV. Turning

I. Compass

I am writing in my second home, as I approach the end of the first half of my life. This designation is only a point of reference, not a signpost. I am writing in a second city and one day when I am not paying attention I find myself at home in Seattle, where the weather is inevitable, a constant if erratic companion instead of a stranger approaching from a distance.

If you stand on the grey-board porch of the house where I grew up, you will find yourself faced with the weather as it comes from the west. El Capitan and Sierra Blanca serve as distance markers, 45.67 and 76.85 miles off, respectively, from Roswell, New Mexico.

I wait with my father who has the habit of witnessing. We face the crisp line of the horizon, watching for the first slow flowering of cumulonimbus. The skin on our faces contracts, the hair lifts on our arms. Hours later, the clouds are leaving our sky, passing over the roof of the house behind us, a slow engine of change. Cholla, ocotillo, and every roadside weed bloom quickly.

I know the smell of rain *phutting* into the dust like some people know the smell of baking bread, that tang that said *ease* and told us to get out of the arroyos.

I inhabit two cities with different weather. Where I am now the rain needles down and we are sewn into weather: there is no clear distinction between the inelegant mud that thrusts up the first shock of crocus and the fog that creeps in under cover of darkness. The wet smells divine. I keep salt cedar twigs on my desk like a bundle of dowsing rods.

In Roswell, the gridline order of streets begins just outside the city limits—it is a city, 35,000-40,000 bodies in 1982, depending on whether or not you are naïve enough to believe the government census. It is a city, though upon leaving we begin to refer to it as a small town, and us, as having grown up in small-town America.

My father and I are standing on a smooth board walkway that paces in regular lengths up to our square front door.

The heavens achieve a sort of wild perfection.

Gathered

The day rose with shivered light, bees braiding a path
before his eye had even opened.

Rose the woman, resonant as a struck cello.

The beekeeper entered his kitchen among the crumbs
from dinner, all taste a light on the tongue.

Blind, but it was only light, bees blurring past, softening
into butter.

He stepped outside the door, entered the patterns among
fireweed, sourwood, goldenrod.

Rose on the balls of his feet, raised his face toward heat
and hum, placed a hand on the hive wall. Found himself

spilled back into the embrace of the woman. Entered
the sound everywhere, gathered like glass, boozy with gold.

Under Heaven

Find a market that sells a pomegranate
in early summer, and you find a place
that doesn't understand how appetite
has a season, how it takes the careful
cultivation of months for its many-chambered
heart to find fullness, a climate both steady and dry
to swell blossoms to galaxies wrapped in taut peel.
What true connoisseur hurries desire
or endures the pith, the grain-grind of seed
absent the anticipation of the small explosion
from the aril that purples the tongue?

Sour Plums

A jackhammer cracks apart concrete slabs.
At the bus stop two girls in hoodies gossip loudly,
curse at traffic. They think they can shock us
as we bend beneath the feral plum tree.
We are in the season of blossoms, white swans
silking the backs of our neck,
dappling our dirty shoes. Next month the tree
will begin to form green fists, hard and destined
to become fruit that is barely edible
but will fatten the squirrels, help the rats
through winter. The spastic boy flails by
in his running suit, and I try to love
the sour flesh of our future,
wonder if given enough sugar the plums
would yield some pleasure, bruised surface
bursting in syrup as I search for the right word
to describe the stone heart and the way it insists
on repeating itself every spring.

Dog Night

Television's "Mister Rogers" died February 27, 2003. On the last show, Rogers... traded his loafers for a pair of... blue sneakers.
    —CNN.com

There's a black dog running
back and forth along this road,
hipbones loose in their sockets, pink
bandana leached gray by the dark.
The mountain gets to its feet and goes walking,
trees bobbing. That we are not shaken
off is amazing, rising in our sleep
to find the world bouncing away
down a long corridor. A bare branch
hangs like wire over the two yellow dog violets
clinging to the bank. In the dark a rush, a roar.
hard to tell the river from the rain.
Fred Rogers dies at seventy-two.
Lets go. Running loose-limbed
like a dumb old dog, no shoes at all.

The Sun Raises Its Axe

but weather slips under
and in moments a pale rain
returning for another listless winter day
dulls the edge which
glances off the wrist
of an idle woman
at an open window
facing an empty street.

Without an umbrella
a walking boy slung low in jeans
looks away from where she watches
at rest within her middle years she
claiming to be free of passion
pulling apart
the crown of a chrysanthemum
love in a golden heap at her feet
falls in a golden heap at his feet
in the space of a moment
between slanting rays.

Interrupt

He is leaving for Tulsa or San Ildefonso Pueblo
in less than fifteen minutes, this kid who wedges
himself, sullen, between a stuccoed blue wall
and three-legged table sweating beneath his glass.
We have come between him and the girl behind the bar.
Maybe he is waiting to take her home. Maybe he is
dreaming of taking her to the dark back room
among bags of beans and jugs of two percent milk
shivering on a chrome refrigerator rack.
Either way he can only watch as her quick wrists
cradle a white ceramic plate of lemon pie.
Her back is to him, spine budding a path
beneath a sweater the color of cantaloupe.
She bends for a clean knife and he hates us.

Rental

Dust sifts through floorboard
gaps, settles along a lintel
that has begun to pull back
from the doorway. Everything
that could be done on the cheap,
by hand, is letting go,
having done enough and more.
Old glass warps and blurs the street
into a torrent of chrome. We've learned
to listen to what the stairs say,
for water in the walls, for mice.
This house eases and groans
under a roof that keeps the two of us,
the cat, and a view of the cedar
flexing and stretching in the wind
for as long as the roots hold.
We can afford agreement
of nail and plaster and wood
to hold, for now, together.

Compass Rose

The cartographer married the exile,
tantalized by the taste of road
when he took her into his mouth,
wanted her, with that wander eye,
as if the last veil
was composed of miles
between them—the revelation
of contour, of gully and incline
in delicate copper, ochre, viridian blue.
She murmurs a litany between
the pillow hours—
Quemado, Puye,
Cebolleta—names he cannot find
on any map,
suspects are old lovers.
It is his delight
to name the constellations crossing
her shoulder
in his own language,
to watch weather
shape them back again
to what she knew,
to what he guesses
her landscape was.

Public Safety Film #217

On the first day of the month, a cloudless afternoon,
it's time for the next in a series of safety films:

What to Do In Case of a Bomb. Mrs. M.
rolls out the projector and flips off the overhead lights.

One kid with a freshly shorn head forms a fist.
The homeroom class is worshipping in slow reptilian shock

the ticking of celluloid looping through a reel, blooming
a bubble of bombs and ash. The girl by the window

curls fetal under her desk, grasping her shoes, listening
to the sound of the world ending. We're all hoping

to be saved, sent out into a day redeemed from disaster,
color bleeding back into tree limbs, the cinder grass.

These are the smells of last days—Tide detergent,
mown grass clinging wetly to our sneakers, Bazooka gum

tucked between cheek and molar. Clasped hands protect
the fracturable spine. We dream a shell, mesmerized

by the way patterns form on the back of the eyelid, sparking
red and gleaming horn. Crouched in our incomprehension,

we wait for the bell's release, turtles softened by the clean
sun, the carotid artery beating tetherball tetherball.

The next day recalling a slow boil of dust
and the way we blew over like wheat in the wind.

Shade Half Drawn

How strange: the only people out, these two
a girl, her aunt or grandmother

strolling
statelier than lilies grow

in weather they make a small crowdedness
for warmth, fly before the rain like chaff

immune to change they come down the block
as they do day after day

in a small pink coat in practical beige
linked by fingers, the walk home from the store

there is no sound
except the shuffle of sensible, rubber-soled shoes,
the tattoo of first heels

lavender along the sidewalk knots
and unknots its fragrance

the light changes around the window,
stretching, the maple shooting skyward

their hands pull apart
and you want to do something

sacrificial, and magnificent, to preserve
those figures under a turning sky that is not on fire

that does not fill with ash, that lowers only fat
snow clouds onto the roofs and ornamental cherries.

Domestic

Leave the sea, return to this more steadfast table;
what is immediate to us is not the tide, ageless
foam, birds beating wings into blades.
The water follows your feet, sea graves

springing up in your footsteps, leaving no path
secret. Come back and you will find your death
asleep by the door, paws folded, bread and onions
on the counter. With its cold voice, the ocean

does not call on you to witness what it knows, shells
cast along a granite-littered coastline. It goes on dying
on a foreign shore in a language you would not recognize.
Turn your back on where it languishes.

Treat with kindness the hound at your foot,
with reverence spill salt onto the plate. It is
the least you can do while you wait for it to rise
from its companionship, becoming something more.

Mare Draws Her Lover Fishing At Dusk

As dark begins to dissolve the body—
the crown of his head, the belly's swell, the ankle—
I watch him sleep, recall how he settled back
on his heels just hours ago, sent a line keening
swift and precise over the lake. Everyone knows
a cast is not a question of strength so much
as a relinquishing, that the line's release
is an extension from the wrist to the lunge
and snap of a Cutthroat Trout. I sketch in the ribbed
trunk of a cottonwood, label it *Populus trichocarpa.*
Something of what the eye took in is translated
to joint and grip of finger, until ink gives back
the crumbled snag of bark, the silver-sided leaf
dipping like a fish through the evening air.
The wing of his hand is the last thing to go.

II. Delicate Work

This morning someone is missing a leg. I have it, wrapped in gauze and several garbage bags, and it reeks. The only sensible thing to do is to drive with my head out the window, dog-like, gasping in clean, scorched air.

This is one of my summer jobs: picking up post-op tissue and fluids from the hospitals to courier them to the lab across town where my father is the chief pathologist. Pathology is the branch of medicine that studies changes in the function and structure of parts of the body to determine the nature and effect of disease. A fraction of the whole tells the larger story. On the front seat of the company car, a lime-green Fiat, I balance a cooler and a plastic carrier tray. A kidney, a section of a lung, and teeth are waiting in labeled specimen containers for examination and diagnosis by a physician.

Later, after work, as plates are clacked and stacked beside the sink my mother draws a noose, and limb by letter we hang either the stick man or his unspoken word. Part by part assembled into a corpus of meaning.

I understand anatomy best in pieces, as components that drive a piston or contract to force oxygen into the mix. The sense of the whole comes mostly through observation and by laying out parts like puzzle tiles, considering what seems to fit, slot to socket, or prodding for the anomaly that affects proper function. I have logged in brain tissue—I'm sure I must have—as well as disparate limbs, laid them out in orderly ranks, to wait for the scalpel's discovery.

As a gift on his fortieth birthday, my father received a knife with its name inscribed on the blade in a varnished box.

I want to tell you what this has taught me.

A reverence for the delicate work of dividing, taking care not to tear the tissue, and a respect for the dual fragility and toughness of the human frame.

That every fragment—from the glass-eyed basalt lava in the Tularosa Valley to beach scree, the granite reduction of mountains licked smooth in the Pacific—articulates the language of the entire. A fox femur found by the river is not wholly fox, but in it is the animal at the margin of a scrub grass field.

A gesture can describe a full motion, the inner eye completing the arc of the swing or stride. And even the loss of a limb or the suspension of the heart's function is a revelation of how the thing works, of the larger word it speaks.

Surviving the Open Heart

The hotel fan's one long drawn exhalation
doesn't disturb the heat that has settled like dust
over the room, the square-cornered chair,
the unsteady spool of table. She is scattered
on its surfaces—a shoe, an unzipped purse
bought cheap for traveling, a scrap of paper
with numbers for St. Joseph's and a sister in Texas.
She has brought changeable clothes, fit to wear
in grief or in joy, comfortable white sandals
with arch support for the waiting, the knit sweater
that draws her husband's eyes to her breasts.

Later she will sink beneath the water of the pool
into a silence as blue as the heart when it stops.
She will practice floating between breaths,
touch two fingers to the place on her abdomen
where tubes left a cave under her father's
sternum and try to imagine how the skin
can keep back what belongs in the dark.
Listening to the twin tides of pulse, she curls
her limbs around her own heart, troubled
by the unthinkable cut, the parting of red wall
upon blue, the delicate machinery suspended.

Day of the Dead

I leave my husband there in Maricopa with its one bank,
one diner, one gas station, to sort through the almost empty
house that I can't bear to face. We'll take what we can use

and forsake the hollow egg collection, a leather glove that
needed a running stitch to close a rent. There's a lacquered box
one of her nieces made, quite ugly, mouth framed by stiffened

Sargent series brushes (No. 8). A mobile of red-crested cranes
eddies and tinks like a quartet of tuneless pianos. Soon we'll be
six states away from where we last broke bread with her.

Down the road a few miles I pull off and pace the trickle
they call a river around here, fading into the ground
in spots like train song. In the language of leaving

there is no returning migration of snow geese,
the peregrination of a red hawk turns
only clockwise, and marigolds come into their own

only on the day of the dead; there is no other color like theirs.
My eye thinks *chromium yellow*. But, perhaps not.
In the grebe's nest among the river-reed bower, in the shroud

of snake skin tossed to the side like a T-shirt at bedtime,
the abandoned speak their half-shape language,
the life gone out of them as it always does.

Prelude to a Drowning

Past four here and the dog
ceases howling at the heat. So little
point to resisting. A brittle thing of blue
light begins its tuning among the trees.
The salt collecting in the elbow's crease
is a part of this, the shade drawn
low on the west side of the house.
Traffic settles in among the gravel drives
and rutted fringes of crab-grass lawns.
If a tentative finger, a silted eye,
catches us unprepared, so what?

Maybe the reservoir hour will hold us under,
drowning among muffled trumpets,
a cathedral rising behind the eyelids,
and with the breath arrested, the tongue
reined in, we can almost begin:
the first throat about to open to dark
and hymning constellations.
From this hour, what comes
is a glimmer across the surface, is
a drowned gavotte between doors, the brush
of a hand against a sleeve like fin over fin.

Preparing For Market

Indifferent from the beginning, the mare
will forget the pinch of the bit,
done with the burden of carrying me.
As the gate closes behind us,

legs cramp from gripping a horse's barrel,
from having ridden for an afternoon
beneath our own star, through air redolent
with offal and dust. Ripe with purpose

we walk the hundred feet back to the house
across gravel, under the press of stars,
drawn toward the smell of potatoes,
following dogs drunk on flushed birds,

on gophers and dung, the retriever bitch
and her pup with the bloody tongues
that have laved our hands and faces.
My body draws back into my coat, waiting

for the tooth to slip free. Even as we master
the horses, drive the calves to the knife,
we are paced and watched and worshipped
by dogs still wolf in the mouth.

Mars hangs a flaming sword to the east.
A bucket splinters into ice. The dark
draws down to cover our tracks, to divide us
from what we have just done.

Compline

Observe how the saddle holds the horse.
See how the girl ascends. She is
memorizing the scars on the mare's back like a map.

As her hands relax, the bit loosens in the tender,
bruised mouth still stained by the last meal.

The mare will carry her
through a pasture ordered by fences
toward an open road. Pasterns bend

in the rhythm of countless horses
before her, a sacrifice of motion.

The gallop crescendos into a shout of praise.
The girl tilts up to where the sun might yet arrive.

As a Flower of the Field

Listen, we have always known—
in this place of grass, in this season
of blazing light—of loss
by fire, of death
by flame. It is as if
we have been waiting all of our lives,
gathering the ephemeral Night-Blooming
Cereus, loving the summer constellations.
Some years the sky is a thickening vine,
fat with water that does not fall. Nevertheless,
in the late hour, in the shadow
of the tilted earth, we come to the table
and fall to our knees. We consume
Orion and the Bear with red sauce and beans
to burn out the taste that sits
in our mouths like an unspoken word.

After Ezekiel

Coming around a bend of the path, we stumble
upon a fox skeleton just this side of the salt cedars,
bullet casings—just two—and the Pecos beyond.

The burr and scratch of sun, the mean catch of wind
finger my spine. I try to move peacefully, hands
empty. And here we pause at the world's dead end

where all hours bide, present in the arrested
bolt of fox toward cover. The bones await
their quickening, flagrant white, beyond the gun.

The body is no longer too hungry to part with.
The river slips past toward the border
of state park land, leaving us behind.

When the wind finds a grass note, what is left
of the animal hisses and crouches for rabbits,
flows after the hot smell of blood. The past

comes back, inspiring the structure of fox.
Both of us face north beside a Russian Olive tree,
a scrim of willow. Relics, we hesitate by the spent

shells and imagine. It is later than when we set out.
I cannot help myself. When we turn to leave I run ahead,
something taking shape at my back, filling with breath.

The Logic of Prayer Rising

If in the detonation of seed, a dandelion,
before it fathers a lawn of sun-headed children,
if at a gesture of wind or the puckered
wish of a girl it undoes itself, then we
in our turn can perhaps be forgiven
a moment of abandon before we part.

And if the pricking berry cane begins to bow
just as it reaches an excess of fruit,
after stretching indiscriminately up the fence
in devotion to the source of light, should it
be possible to remain mute before need,
desire spiraling and seeking?

If air in its extremity visibly ascends
off the hot hood of a blue Ford, if a tat
of flies spins into ecstasy in a draft
from the open window, then the tongue
curls to the mouth's bruised roof,
the body rises also on knees and an elbow.

Annunciation: Triptych

I.

The half moon caught in the orange tree
swaying, a slant husk on the windowsill
facing the Dead Sea. Who can say what
embodies a vessel? What strange messenger
finds his way between limb and the leaf-cast
shadow, filling the hollow clay?

II.

Waking, I begin to shape a bowl large enough
to hold three blood oranges still in their rind.
The lip curls like the crest of a dune
where wind leaps back into air's embrace.
It may take months to find the particular language
of the wheel, letting the silk of clay cover my hands.
All the time filling up, becoming less and less Mary.

III.

My bed is empty, lamp blown. Sharp and acidic,
I taste him among the peculiar appetite of night,
taste him like the salt of the sea
miles from this room. I miss Joseph,
who has gone back to board and nails,
closed to these arms. Though hollow as a bowl
inside, I am vast and humming.

At the Gate

Across the street a peach tree crabs and lifts a scant
handful of yellow fruit and the snake is back,
lisping. I pause but can't make out the words.

Low clouds suffocate the neighborhood, weather
change bruising the bay blue. Down this road
a dog has been beaten, cursed, not called Sugar.

Down that driveway, behind the fence, a window
shatters, a woman cries through bitten lips.
The splintered sound stays with me all day.

Then he comes stealing home, gathers the pieces,
draws to himself the bridge of a rib, fingers tapping out
Morse code for *sweet as honey, ice queen, Eve.*

To the gate of my mouth he lifts
a segment of Satsuma and tartness radiates
across my palate, burns down my throat.

You Ask Again If I Am Well

And I'll admit it's true that

sometimes I sit before the television all static
glow and flicker. Not one thing looks back at me.
      Other days,

ghosting down the corridor, aching like a sour tooth.

On Channel 1, a woman fat as a milk-fed cat and bloated
as a spoon in August stirs up trouble:
      everybody sees her.

Could I amount to anything, subtracted as I am?

There's a prison break on Channel 4; I slip between
the bare ribs of a cell unnoticed. How would it feel I wonder
      to stick between the teeth?

The phone is ringing in the walls around me

the people in the room next door most visible and loud.
A thumbprint marks us all, a fixed and stubborn map
      you cannot alter, but

the flesh at least can be renounced, a seam pulled tighter.

I keep myself—listen, there are things one guards against
—private. I prefer to eat alone. Here I am concrete, here
      obscured. I invert

the mirror or is it me that turns, the face forgotten? Both
lost and found, I move my palm over the clavicle,
      the jut of the ileum crest,

the telling prayer of presence on the rosary of the spine.

This Has Been a Summer of Moths

As if born the moment
we opened to the dark,
as if they'd been breeding
behind thyme, the tin of Earl Grey,

silver slips rise
from a bed of linen,
from damp-scented woolens.
Drifting out of cupboard doors

unsunned and not called
to any lit flame,
it took a week to determine
a scattered flock

instead of one soft ash
resurrected again and again.
Shivering somnambulists
baffled by glass, they die for lack.

They go to dust
on the windowsill, a wing fading
to a translucent brown sail, prepared
around the absence of body.

The Snow Globe Repairman

Crawford looks at his hands with their knuckles like tectonic
plates, cradling a seeping globe that encloses

the Pyramids of Giza. Like his wife's breast
and the frayed head of the old retriever. So much

the same, how they fit within his palm. In a glass
cupola, vees of geese tilt north past New York City,

the Peace Arch and hula girls sway in a slurried snow.
They all come to him here; every dreamt destination,

every journey's souvenir lies unwrapped, nested in
a newspaper from Poughkeepsie or brown parchment.

What a woman wants to preserve of the grotto at the Bay
of Conca Dei Marini rests in a tangle of pliers and glue,

tubes of glitter in gold, silver, and the occasional blue.
He knows something of purity's formula, can mix up water

sweet enough not to cloud or green. He examines a curve
for imperfection, a flaw like a mar on a peach that needs

the tender knife. And although this particular day he enters
the workshop more slowly, and cups heat first in a fist

to limber up stiff joints, he recalls well enough
similar evenings when the light was going, when she waited

for him to finish. How her voice traveled across the field
as she called him home for dinner. They spoke of Paris

at the orchard gate. He stretches tendons for the delicate
work of repair, heaven's dome fixed securely above.

III. How to Fall

The hour is late. Delridge is strange in its flood of shadows and I am once again in the company of sleepwalkers and insomniacs. My tired eyes won't make sense of a white form that slips between parked cars.

On my way to the 24-Hour L'il Mart, I imagine that behind each front door there's a sleeper. Or worse, I find myself thinking that down the block, all along Holden Street, hundreds of others stare at the ceiling, clapped in by roofs and wires without the solace of the stars, that we all lie adrift, too listless to compose or sort out, too uninspired to create.

Sleep has not always been so elusive. In 1985, after the graveyard shift at Eastern New Mexico Medical Center, I'd simply drop onto the mattress on the apartment floor. All the blinds were up. Sand-laden wind scrubbed at the window and in spite of the heat, both cats slept by my side and we rode the sound like we were slaloming through dry snow; that same wind once stripped an earring from my left ear.

These days, if I feel the creeping chemical change that presages a restless night, I am prone to panic a little.

Some rituals developed by insomniacs seem ridiculously elaborate. We wield them like charms to compel the waking, circadian rhythm to relinquish the field to the night brain. Lavender pillow spray, oil rubbed on the temples, the recorded call of a loon. Blackout shades and foam earplugs. Spelling short common words backwards. Counting down from 100, or 1000, depending on how bad you have it. A shot of brandy in warm milk. Valerian, calcium, chamomile.

I used to hope for at least the bent clarity that comes to some people at 2 a.m. A kind of ecstatic trance or a moment when inspiration drags herself through the subconscious, sends a poet stumbling through ranks of daffodils.

In the meantime, there is a kind of compensation that comes at that hour—an acuteness of the senses found at the edge of deprivation. Every footfall coming down the sidewalk is portentous. The car that runs past the door carries a specific woman who's taken off her pearl pendant and slung her kitten heels onto the passenger seat. No one is merely a commuter, a part of the body count of day drivers.

Tonight, there's a Hunger Moon. The honeycomb pleats of the blackout blinds—a concession to the fire station's relentlessly-lit parking lot—are contracted and I stretch out beside the open window. One streetlight has failed to ignite on Fremont, leaving the heavens undimmed. The forsythia provides a delicate sift of shadow. With a good run of sleep behind me, I get cocky. Tonight I intend to sleep under the moon, wooing a measure of madness. I think, *maybe tonight, epiphany.*

The Bearded Lady, Asleep

She rests her pretty curls,
white cotton gloves upon
her hands. She sleeps secure
and does not miss the dawn,
fallen sparrow in God's palm.
The hairs on her face so

delicate. And the Lord
who created her, who knew
her in her mother's womb,
cradles her head in time.
Soft the tents are struck, soft
the evening clocks, chiming,
from her pillow singing,
rising from her pillow's dream.

Open to the evening,
untangling locks and knots
of beard, she is known of God,
chosen Adam, chosen
Eve, knows he makes them
in his mirror, female.
Male. He makes them her. His
glory is in her hair. Listen
for her off-key humming.

A Case for Insomnia

Another night has come another hour
when a raccoon has sorted all the refuse
when the flickering streetlight steadies
and black blooms out from its golden eye.

It is in this hour that you experience joy
though perhaps not recognizing it
in the sidewalk beneath the trembling
of the dogwood as it combs light
and shadow, shadow across your window.

A cup of tea is steeping, or maybe brandy
burns the throat. Maybe you have
risen from a bad dream
shocked by the cold floor into waking. Maybe
you have risen at the sound of the street sweeper
alone in her bright machine, tracing the bones of the city.

And even if it is grief that lifts your head
from the pillow, a space left empty
beside you, you can still taste
the way the night holds everything in its mouth
savored and cold like the ice cube
dropped into the glass with its perfect chime.

Haint

In the highway's curve, in the swept
light that precedes the car, I am
coming home. I imagine you
safe, enfolded in the blue quilt.
I know you'll have left a lamp lit
as a pact with the fear I have
of stumbling, of entering the house
asleep to find no one I recognize.
I pull the wheel against the gravel's slide.
There are more and more moments like this:
the key hesitates in the lock and I cannot
remember what side of the night I travel on.

How Water Folds Over

All I can recall when opening eyes to dark
so thick that it made opening useless,
is a flickering image. I dreamt you swimming

the air (oddly viscous like amber),
mouth agape, suspended
between words. Awake, I find myself

thinking of summer lessons preserved
in neon blue, watched as we practiced, moving
down lanes with rigid arms rowing,

rowing, first the chemical air
then the deep below us dim
as REM sleep. Even a wild thrashing

can keep a swimmer afloat.
The danger lies in not moving at all, legs
dropping like dumb bell clappers. Another night

it was Moses standing muddy footed
at the side of the pool, about to enter
with his staff raised. I wanted to shout

that it was not enough, that one deliberate blow,
however perfect his form. What was needed
was an understanding of grace and the act

of repetition. I wanted him to taste the taste
of chlorine, water entering the mouth, stopping
the ears as I lost track of the concrete brink

because no one had told me
how water could fold over some and not others,
depending on practice and blood and who stood

on the bank. But I could not enter back into the dream.
So tonight I reach across to where your arms drag
deep and weighted in sleep, and begin

to move them as the lifeguard moved our limbs
in the shallow end, teaching muscle to work with the water,
to compel the whole body flailing or not toward shore.

Insomnia on Aurora Avenue

I.

Morning arrives late in winter, lingers on black paint
across the window of Sugar's Nite Club.
Even the rain moves aside to the curb—
the sun has every place to lay its hands.

ll.

I am the witness of the dawn.
The sun rising is not the echo of another sun rising.
Nor is it new born,
but swings 'round the east, opening wider
its yellow eye. The illumination and shadow cast
across the Chrysler lot are equally sharp.
I have stood before a car in its flaunt of chrome and seen God
as an attendant outside the Shell station
unfolds a sign board, smoothing her stained overalls.

North on the Illahee Ferry

So there you are, where you wanted to be.
I can imagine the Seattle city pier falling away
behind you. Herring gulls wheel along their wires,
reflections shattering in the ferry wake. You lean out

over the swell, caught by blue distance, and when
the cold finds its way onto the deck, plunder a pocket
for an orange and break the body into crescent-shaped
pieces brought in a wooden cage over the pass

from their God-hung green night. Teeth tear membrane
as the coastline recedes. North is sudden and near,
the final island before dark. Urgently the senses surge
toward Texas, parts south where an orchard yields

the finite sun over and over again, where once
someone loved you. Swallow what reminds you of home.
What's held in both hands and the limitless motion
you longed for and only dimly understand—love,

the same thing sustains them, the vastness
that's kept you and indeed everyone on the vessel afloat.
And at this table where a letter has reached us,
is being read and reread, we are nearly present on the boat,
when both citrus and the salt season the moment.

Thrift

Me? No, I have never wrung the velvet necks
of the wild guinea hens that in leaner days

graced Grandma Martin's table,
felt pebbled skin cool

stripped of all that is soft and fine,
have never tasted boiled squirrel.

On the mantel, there's a clutter of snapshots
brimming with cousins and kids in their ill-fitting best.

Here's three generations outside Mount Vernon, eyes
cast down toward the Potomac. Grandma clutches

my mother's shoulder, our shoulders. Each woman's dress
is cut down or altered from someone else's cloth.

I suspect several more generations of girls will grow fat
on this thin broth, the measure of thrift and enough,

the litany of a button saved—
rubbed down to wafer thinness—

that sometimes spills from my own tongue.
At breakfast my niece complains about the portions

though I mean to be generous here. It's sometimes
true I begrudge the squirrel the sunflower seeds

the cardinal likes, that flagrant bird, and I like watching
—maybe this makes me frivolous. I am freer

with the stale bread and the seed mix, and
anticipate the scattered flax that comes up

spindly in the following spring, with its slight blue bloom.
And though I may not see them, I like to think

there are sparrows uncounted entering the atmosphere
fed on the crusts, crops gorged with what we let fall.

Summons

When adolescence came to her daughters, her legs
locked together as theirs loosened.
They had already begun to leave, stopping their ears,

migrating. Yet they turned back, not knowing
whether to eat, to fatten or famine, all plenty suspect.
Where could they have gone, anyway,

far enough not to hear? As her mother kept her
bound to the dinner bell on a post by the back door,
helplessly tuned she rang them, hand on iron clapper,

on twisting rope. In their dark caves, they swung
passive as bats in daylight. In the hour between meals,
a moon sweetened and surrendered its innocence

to the vulgar magpie. They spun, whispering together,
dreaming of the world winged and thirsting. Wanting to be
struck again, themselves the only thing resounding.

Resolutions

Wear nonsensical heels   investigate the suspicion of doubt
spend more time gathering stones   date a baker and learn to
taste the difference in flours   impress vermilion upon a lip
emulate spiders: touch everything first before engaging
ask to be called Jane   collect Janes   paint the bathroom black
memorize a Basho poem that is not about leaving   call your
mother only when half-drunk   have an icon of Teresa of Avila
beside you when you call   study walls, what they keep in
eat some animal you've never seen   draw what that animal
tastes like   clean out the deep freeze in the basement
call your mother Elizabeth as if by mistake   attend a
Beekeepers of America meeting   read a biography about
Amelia Earhart   change the cat's name to Amelia   dream of
Icarus   pray beneath low ceilings. Maybe then.

Immolation

As the horizon looms, flips over to present
an endless span of waves, I give up, surrender.
My fate's the fate of falling. I guess I hoped for recognition,
that when I pushed my arms into the hostile sun
he would look up and see my face, the frame
of limb so like his lover, perhaps invoke my name.

I imagine women fainting at the thought
of this lovely form's ravagement, the taint
of char hot enough to warp a wooden strut,
melt wax, and singe. But Daedelus flies on.
The body will soften momentarily, pliable if heavy,
finding shape hours later, so I devise my final self.

The scent surely travels downwind
in the contrail of smoke he, at least, could see.
I thought he'd catch me; if nothing else
to save the contraption with its maze
of gears and levered joints. I counted on,
I understood, he loved the thing.

Icarus' Gift

Upon waking, above me a sky so open,
half stunned I stretched beneath
constellations; Amelia was humming
over a small campfire meal.
There was no father I wanted
to please, in my memory, no mother.

This woman knows no other man
who has survived such falling. Whatever
was damaged is attributed
to the envious sun, is now
ash. To remember that rising and the flail
of wings failing
did not wake me last night for once.

Sleeping in Grandmother Wolfe's House

Buried here in sheets in this darkened room,
sometimes time sits heavy on the soul.
Some evenings with a last over-the-shudder
look out the window, Red finds herself receding
further, further back, to stone, becoming
the dead thing that fell from the branch,
or the bird-bitten, unplucked callow drupe.

This is the bed where she was born.
The mirror tipped in its walnut frame pins her
flat against the wall, same axe-blade face
suspended there above a crocheted doily
that her grandmother saw, that woman
whose knife pared each portion to its core,
the crevassed heart of apricot and plum.

Red #9

a handful of wolves
all cream pelts and sloping shoulders
appear with girls in red, jaws
snapping like capes;
    with silver spoons the girls eat the air
grow teeth the size of axes

there is something you like
in this dream—
    grasses parting like
                the sea before Moses
a sense of law in the way wolves run
through the hissing waver

the girls are
not
    the wolves' dream—
they vanish
into feather beds
when the pillow is turned over

The Very Air That Midas Takes In Gleams

At last, the feral red deer is stopped,
frozen just before her lips—no longer soft—
closed upon the cream-colored loft

of roses, the tender skirts of lettuce.
Knowing the arbor is safe, inviolate,
that an immaculate bloom will always grace

his table in a golden vessel, he finds her almost
beautiful. The outstretched neck, the exposed
throat and gilded flank his daughter longed

to stroke. She's a different creature now
—without her swiftness, without the shying hoof,
only the impenetrable heart preserved.

Prospect

There's that metal taste across my tongue
again. The silver shafts of rain descend.
The mouth recognizes both vinegar and blood.
Lingua sour mixes pain and piety in the dim within.
The stained thick glass thinly sieves the view outside.
The graveyard's aspect enters in
nonetheless. It rings the bell's insistent tongue.

IV. Turning

At the observatory, before the lights go off, I note that construction seams are hidden by a good paint job. This is important for an umblemished view. I choose a seat in the sweet spot of this more modern, tilted dome, here for the revelation of the perfect night sky unhindered by the afternoon's sun.

Halfway around the world is the sky from which Icarus mythically fell, undone by that same sun. Amelia Earhart too has fallen out of history. What we remember best are their endings. But, for me, any lament about mechanical failure or human hubris is subsumed by a frisson of awe. Part of what pulls me out from under my roof at dusk, star chart in hand, is this. Their disastrous descents mean that the myth, the made thing, and the aviatrix once ascended, rowed heavenward into thinning air before they plummeted to terra firma.

The Robert H. Goddard Planetarium I visited as a kid is housed in the same building as the local art museum. Henriette Wyeth and Peter Hurd depict the stark loveliness of the Hondo Valley and hang next door to the Carina Nebula—work that is seriously heliocentric back-to-back with a geocentric view of the universe.

The creator who kindled the sun and rolled satellite moons into pearls also undoes the envelope of a late-evolved star and tips minute grains of cosmic dust out into space.

A domed ceiling models the movement of the heavens. No one can take in the entire observable universe in one visit. This afternoon we fix our gaze on the autumn sky over the northern hemisphere—a collection of icy pinpricks.

Making a telescope of my hands, I choose one of The Three Sisters, deciding this will be the low-voiced star I seek out later, in the hazed October evening.

The air outside is thick with cosmic debris. A meteorite thunks down into the ocean, dragging an aggregate of dust in its wake. Elsewhere, cosmic dust drifts earthward to settle across an iceberg in Greenland. The body of the boy tearing tags of paper from his notebook in the seat beside mine contains the same elements as that debris; he is comprised of stardust. Stars, falling out of the immense, into the particular.

These days, I'm plugged into Spaceweather Radio, which follows Air Force Space Surveillance Radar as it sweeps the skies over Texas. It provides white noise while I work, mostly, a static rush like tires over tarmac. Occasionally there's a ping. Something arrives: a satellite blinking like a double star, or a conflagration of matter hurtling toward the quenching sea. A presence, a piece of the vastness, has entered the atmosphere. I look up to take it in.

Deconstruct

After the last discussion Annette resolves not to wear words while he's gone, cuts his t-shirts from the Ashland Festival and the Neil Young Harvest Moon Tour into rags for the rag drawer. She keeps the Harley-Davidson because that was his favorite and looks better on her and besides the print was small, wings that catch the eye flashing across her right breast, reminding her of county two-lanes, the sharp sour pleasure of diner coffee drunk under neon. Lately he wears shirts that only say things that make no sense to her, like the green one with a gorilla toting guns, "Engine Kid" arcing over its head. Nothing gets resolved. Now here she is with a silent wardrobe, scissors in hand, a pile of cotton strips swaddling her feet.

Edges

An ear's rim, the hem of rain preceding a storm,
the cavity carved by a mouth's embrace
of apple meat, she loves it all—the sharp,

the keen. A green-broke horse under the saddle,
the crooked wound of a lover's kiss,
a granite bluff dropping away beneath dirty feet,

even the cheek laid open with surgical precision,
the fist cleaving the space between them.
There's the barred shade left by the venetian blinds,

the intersection between Christ the Redeemer
and Girls Girls Girls, the impossible silhouette
of the Bitterroot Range strung like barbed wire

across Montana. And some days all she wants to be
is a county road arcing away from electricity, past
fallow hay fields, on the brink of the blind curve.

If It Doesn't Rain Soon

You eat without light, a hand gripped around a knife;
the shade is drawn against the sun. Beyond,
a man, a paper sack of smokes and onions,
scrapes along the sidewalk. Metro hunches north.

Traffic shakes loose Sugar's, Blue Moon Video,
the XXX Lounge. A woman slumps
in a plastic lawn chair, spread legs
bracketing a dog with a head like a shovel.

Next door the fire station wails in the heat.
Large hands slap a heavy hose into glistening coils.
The hope of something happening, of someone
entering the stifling house, who can sustain it?

Yesterday a neighbor sat at the kitchen table
watching the water ring left by a half-full glass
evaporate; now she's gone. You, you love it,
this lethargy with only the press of heat

to push against. You longed for the cessation of rain,
but, you think when the evening comes
you will go outside into the yard that you know
even in the dark and pray for the weather to ease.

Scar

And surely now you can understand
the consequence of meeting
separation with stubborn intent
to mend, to build a fence, seaming
what was rent from what was rent.
The flesh does not forget
the cut. I feel along the scar.

The marred surface writes me different
from anybody else. You never really
know how proud the flesh can be
until it fails to keep and forms a fist.
Admit it, sometimes it's best to leave alone
the damage done. You surely never meant
to leave a telling mark. And still,

after the parting of the flesh, you cannot help
but love the knot that stitched it whole.
The nervous friction of a touch excites
the catch of skin, the dance of sinew over bones.

Oration

In St. Mary's Cemetery in Missoula, Richard Hugo walks
among the headstones; his own ghost meets him there.

He scrolls the names, speaks of *a sister sleeping, the sweetest
    flower,*
wets his lips, begins again to recite the strange and the familiar,

giving each a living resonance. The tongue as well as the pen
can honor structure long after it's dust, he surmises,

though the pool of an eye fills up and the air crackles
with an elemental static from that strange conversion back to
    dust.

Some granite slabs tilt or sag, others more deeply sunk
have lapsed beneath a yew's skirt, illegible. It's impossible
    to know

if his pronunciation hits the mark, but who's to say? His mouth
still full of German women, he stops to rest his feet. Is that

his porch light down the hill, his place of—what—of rest?
Should he go home? He thinks about promises made

to lovers and his students, those gone to bed, untroubled
in the night. Does it matter if there is more he needs

to say? He doesn't know. Below, among their unconscious
    breath's
small ceasings they compose themselves, exhale a last *I am.*

Soufflé

As instructed he has separated the eggs while cold,
easing the whites from the yolk. Next,
fold gently by hand: the meaning obvious
only to one who spends time in the kitchen coddling
or beating till smooth, and sculpting peaks of meringue

from a little sugar, a pinch of cream of tartar.
He comes to it innocently, offering to bake the thing,
to pull together the list of ingredients—he knows
how to measure, thinks of a pinch as the fold
he grabs between forefinger and thumb,

slightly loose, on the underside of her arm.
Like the skin of a concord grape just past its prime
he says, not understanding why she slaps
at his hand. Because they have collected farm-fresh
eggs from the Saturday market, because he is still

addled from how she moves between the produce
stalls, shopping basket bumping the swell of her hip
that he layered beneath his own not hours ago,
he offers to prepare a dish, asks
what she wants and finds himself, the uninitiated,

thinking only of folding one body beneath another.
This is in his mind as he cooks and he expects
an alchemy of air and batter to result in loft. Is bewildered
by what comes out what, she insists they eat. She wolfs
each quiver of soufflé, flat, glistening, and sweet.

Men Who Love the Domed Heads of Old Dogs

whose hands like thick pads
polish the half-globe
from white fringed brow
to nape, those
are the men I love
who move gentle
slowly folding knees
offering homage
to the fine silk of an ear,
loving the large
nature, the teeth
that slumber behind slack lips.

Beats Working for a Living

She thinks, so the poet tries her hand at romance fiction.
It's better done under a dramatic sky or circumstance
she understands and gets to it.
A slip of the hand turns page into prose.
A negligee appears, a laddered hose. Stripped,
apparently the body knows to let things ride.
The corporal exits on his horse without regret.

Awaiting Arrival

After all these years of nothing coming
down the road, she still preserves lemons,
still salts fish and leaves the door unlocked
to the winter traveler. In the pantry
among the Ryvita rye and sesame crackers,
there are rooted things in abundance:
the fat pearl of Walla Walla sweet onions,
the folded wings of garlic, each shrouded
in tissue paper. She, like all her neighbors,
keeps the freezer stocked with zucchini bread
and coffee in case of the improbable arrival
of snow or the advent of a stranger, each visitation
anticipated like a bridegroom a long time coming.

Idle

The dark cat points north, the other
watches the trail left by the sun
and hopes for fat squirrels. Anyone
can play in the devil's playground when
winter lies about the imminent arrival
of robins. If deadlines come tomorrow
and not today. An oil truck idles
at the traffic signal. Shivering, the windows
press unbloomed daphne and white lilac
against their faces. A twist of wind
and something striking the pane startles
both cats and we gather to peer through
and down at unmowed grass and wonder if this
is portent. Cannot decide if a storm-shed branch
or a wren marked by God would be more
disturbing. Nothing rises from the lawn.

Whalefall

After a long day of rain, we settle in to watch *Planet Earth*.
The screen darkens, sediment like scree cascades
through the abyssal plain's night, spot lit by an underwater
camera. The Belgian research team is leaning in,
as I am leaning in. The narrator has told us what to expect:

a whale carcass has come to rest on an ocean shelf,
an extended feast for the cusk eel and hadal snailfish.
It is the fat that's the last putrefying thing to go
unless you count the skeleton, a keeled-over ship-frame
that the current sucks and strokes. And even that,

the Osedax disarticulates, the worm rooting in the bone
and finding what will nourish. Sinew is gone, all connecting
tissue swallowed or gnawed, the last sour string
of muscle clawed free of mooring. Like the tooth,
all tools of edge and scrape have done their work.

In another time zone, at the breakfast table, my cousin
has peeled the fragile velvet from an Elberta peach
        for his daughter
and watches her cradle the wet flesh and eat it down
to the pit, that stubborn abiding fragment of whole.

So You Think You're Odd

So you think you're odd, doubly blessed
with two left feet and genetically inclined toward
facial hair. When you lean close, spittle sprays;
someone hands you a pink plastic mirror that proves
white stuff gathers at the corners of your mouth
even when you keep it shut. You'll improperly substitute
strophe for stanza at a writers conference. The UFOs
that cross your sky elude the telescopes of others.
Between the library stacks you shuffle, fishing
for a book on Alpine sheep. A hum rises in your throat,
ascends to a yodel, or something worse. You wonder
who asks a person to enter all that language and be mute?
A troll would love your chin, underslung and knobby.
And like the box fish, your shape repels predators
—even those you think you'd like to date; you wouldn't
fit into their barrel-shaped jaws, you lucky thing.
Why hide the shape you're in, when it keeps you
out of danger? Why join the rank of sardines
that slouch toward an exit? Tell the truth, you'd rather
fall in love with a harlequin shrimp, anyway,
or join the kids at the tidal touch pool where the strange
can sometimes happen: before it extends its cardia
stomach to taste you, the beaded bubbled digits
of the Short-spined Sea Star stroke and sting your knuckles.

Envying Snow

Last night I called my brother back east
who's stalled deep in snow. At least
he has the profligate pleasure of his dog
plowing white hummocks with her nose. He says
his second daughter gives each unsullied drift
grave consideration before plunging in. In our yard,
the crocuses ignite, the barberry sheaths thorn
teeth in chartreuse. Such a relief, this change,
even for you, used to the perpetual grey, this moving
off and away of winter's cumulonimbus threat of sleet.

Beneath us the microbes and root threads teem—
the dirt is coming awake from its sodden dream.
I think we're expected to celebrate this visible
surge of life. However, I turn like Lot's wife back
to when last month's storm stripped naked
the architecture of the Crimson Glory vine,
to how you grasped my hand to counterbalance,
and the way we took the loss of certainty.
Deliberate and so tender with each step
cutting through the thin, crisp ice.

Leda

My sister tells a story about a swan and a jeweled strand.
I have never thought of myself as a bird before.
A heron stabs after the half moon among the current,
then lifts off, carving into the horizon.
The sea shirs the sand where my foot rests.
Caught in the mirror, her daughter blooms pale,
hung from the morning like a pearl pendant.

In the Heat of the Summer

Namibian desert lions, driven out
to the Skeleton Coast to survive on whales,
cormorants, seals, had all but disappeared.

The lion wind, having exhausted
its tawny breath, lithes among grass

fattening to seed and bending,
praying to unburden itself of fruit.

The lion wind invites the sun to the edge
of shade and says, listen

I have traveled beyond the Skeleton Coast
and it is enough to die here

everything swallowed,
like distance, in the heat of the summer.

Random Airport Autobiography #5

Not so long, or far, since we knew such wide skies
The atmosphere's
    Lid blown off and guttering away across the horizon

In the mouth of rain, a tension,
Each drop biting into the tarmac

It may always be like this:
    A difficult sky, the bend of the earth hidden

        Before the windowed waiting room
      Beyond the shuddering plane

Late Night in Neon

I have eaten the flesh of baigai, small water snails;
they were exquisite in their brine of vinegar
and smooth as glass. Savory fluke fins cross
your lips, devoured with red pickled ginger
and thinly sliced gari to cleanse the palate.
We have tongued up pearls of tobiko.
It is time to go. Mouths sleepy, heads low,
we swim out beneath the hiss of noble gases.

At the end of the block, there's one diner, still open.
A neon clock has stopped at nearly two a.m.,
the second hand gliding across the window
of a passing car like motor oil. No one tries
the door, or starts away from the hung bell clamor.
Out of sight, the cook eases down onto a low
slump of rice sacks and cardboard boxes.
The hour pulls its raincoat closer.

I watch the neon's fitful flame
coil around your neck, your wrist. Our bones,
light blind, are speaking, the way cuttlefish
in flagrante, fathoms deep, coalesce and strobe
beneath the ocean's lid, beneath the sperm whale
groaning in her sleep. The tender meat of appetite
manipulates the iris, lens, and shutter, persuades
the traveler to a single pyrotechnic meeting.

In the extra dark the rain provides,
an old woman rises and finds the blind
cord, leans her forehead against the pane.
The fluorescing sign for Mioki's Sushi Bar—
now closed—meteors across the room,
kindles every edge and curve, the orange cat's eye,
a bioluminescent blending with the fitful night
outside. On the wet sidewalk, only you and I.

Kaleidoscope: it takes so little to alter history
It can all be done with a thumb

Acknowledgements

First, my deepest appreciation to Jeffrey for his unflagging support and love, for the miles covered together, and for the hours spent side by side, bent over the page.

To Laura Barkat and Marcus Goodyear for the opportunity and for the enthusiasm that made this project such a pleasure.

To Scott Cairns who gifted me with his time and counsel, both of which I value greatly.

To all the members of the Meridian Poets, former and current, but most especially Marjorie Manwaring, Jody Zorgdrager, Nicole Hardy, Arlene Kim, Carol Kelly, and Hannah Notess. And to my extended writing community, Tara Owens, Bob Denst, and Letitia Montgomery-Rogers.

To my family, the Does and the Overstreets and Morrises. But especially to my sister Kathie and to Lois and her Monday prayer group.

To Vivian Bennett and Tommy Fong who have been faithful friends and a constant source of support.

And finally, to Luci Shaw, Anastasia Solano, Derek Sheffield, and Linda Wagner whose inspiration, steady encouragement, and example make me a better writer.

About the Poet

Anne M. Doe Overstreet's work has been published, or is forthcoming, in *Asheville Poetry Review, Nimrod International Journal of Prose and Poetry, Radix, DMQ Review, Relief, Talking River Review, Cranky, The Mendon-Honeoye Sentinel,* and *thematthewshouseproject.com.* Her poetry has also been featured in the Seattle City Council's *Words Worth* program and has appeared as part of the Cody Center Exhibition "Pairings" at Laity Lodge in Texas.

She is a Soapstone Resident and a two-time Pushcart Prize nominee. She has conducted workshops locally on, among other things, "Persevering in Poetry: How to Develop a Life-Long Habit." After having spent her formative years in Roswell, New Mexico, she now resides just north of Seattle with her husband Jeffrey Overstreet and earns her keep as a freelance editor and private gardener.

Also from T. S. Poetry Press

***Barbies at Communion: and Other Poems,*
by Marcus Goodyear** (**Best Poetry Book 2010 Runner
Up,** *Englewood Review of Books*)

Marcus Goodyear's poems are portable, easily carried in the
mind, tightly compressed and deceptively simple, like a capacious
tent folded into a package you can tuck in your backpack.

— John Wilson, Editor, *Books & Culture*

From Barbies to tea bags and credit cards, from broken pipes to
communion wafers and mowing dead grass, Marcus Goodyear
moves us through our world. His juxtapositions of the conven-
tionally sacred and profane reveal to us the falsness of our
conventions. Where the vision is large, all is sacred.

— John Leax, author *Tabloid News*

***God in the Yard: Spiritual Practice for the Rest of Us,*
by L.L. Barkat**

Mix Richard Foster and Annie Dillard in a blender, and you'll
pour out *God in the Yard...*

— Ginger Kolbaba, editor Christianity Today's *Kyria*

L.L. Barkat's wise words move us more deeply into matters of
consequence.

— David Naugle, author *Reordered Love, Reordered Lives: Learning the
Deep Meaning of Happiness*

Neruda's Memoirs: Poems,
by Maureen E. Doallas

Lyrical, poignant and thought-provoking, *Neruda's Memoirs* is a stunning collection which brings us closer to the truth.

— Deborah Henry, Historical Fiction Finalist at *Solander Magazine*

Maureen Doallas's poems delight us with the play of words and impress us with their struggle, to make sense of nature and our natures. Like "stars splitting the dark," they shine on faith, on the treasures of this world, and on their long-grieving loss.

— A. Jay Adler, Professor of English at Los Angeles Southwest College

Contingency Plans: Poems,
by David K. Wheeler (Finalist, Indie Booksellers Choice Awards, 2011)

A great poet confounds me; he uses the same materials I do — words — but where I've built a fort, he has erected a cathedral. Wheeler has "revealed the space behind our ribs," and I must remove my sandals.

— Susan Isaacs, author of *Angry Conversations with God*

Infused with the sort of holiness discovered in that quiet place behind the mighty waterfall, or staring straight up into the outstretched arms of a Ponderosa pine.

— Karen Spears Zacharias, author *Will Jesus Buy Me a Double-Wide?*

All T. S. Poetry Press titles are available online in e-book and print editions. Print editions also available through Ingram.

Follow T. S. Poetry Press on Facebook at
http://www.facebook.com/pages/T-S-Poetry-
Press/149822048417893

Made in the USA
Lexington, KY
30 June 2011